The Chester Books of Madrig

3. DESIRABLE WOMEN

Edited by Anthony G. Petti

For Jeremy

CONTENTS

Chester Music

Cover:
May (Taurus/Gemini) from the
Très Riches Heures du Duc de Berry.
Reproduced by kind permission of the Musée Condé, Chantilly.

1. TRAUT MARLE

1. "Marle, my pretty, drive the geese into the sweet peas for me." "Certainly not, you can go choke yourself, 'cause the one who drives them in has to take them out again, pom, tiddly, pom. Don't give me no trouble, for that's the story of my life, pom, tiddly, pom."

2. "Marle, my pretty, drive the geese into the beets for me." "Not on your life. I'm frightened of big boys like you, 'cause the one who drives them in has to take them out again, pom, tiddly, pom. Don't give me no trouble. . . "

Anon. (German, early 16th century)

15
wie - der auss - - her. Her - um pum pum, und
treib dir's wie - der auss - her. Her - um pum pum, her - um pum pum, und
treib dir's wie - der auss - her. Her - um pum pum, und
treib dir's wie - der auss - her. Her - um pum pum, her - um pum pum, und
staccato
mf
p
mp
20
mach kein Krumm, ich bitt dich all mein Leb - tag drum, her - um pum
mach kein Krumm, ich bitt dich all mein Leb - tag drum, her - um pum pum,
mach kein Krumm, ich bitt dich all mein Leb - tag drum, her - um pum
mach kein Krumm, ich bitt dich all mein Leb - tag drum, her - um pum pum,
25
pum, und mach kein Krumm, ich bitt dich all mein Leb - tag drum!"
her - um pum pum, und mach kein Krumm, ich bitt dich all mein Leb - tag drum!"
pum, und mach kein Krumm, ich bitt dich all mein Leb - tag drum!"
her - um pum pum, und mach kein Krumm, ich bitt dich all mein Leb - tag drum!"
V. 2 poco rall.
f

2. MARFIRA, POR VOS MUERO

Marfira, I am dying for love of you, and Love can swear that I endure my pain happily and in silence. See how strong my grief is, since to be silent is death to me, though I also hold this as a benefit. But I carry you in my breast, and you know that you have set it on fire. I should like, without speaking, to be understood.

Anon. (Spanish, early 16th century)

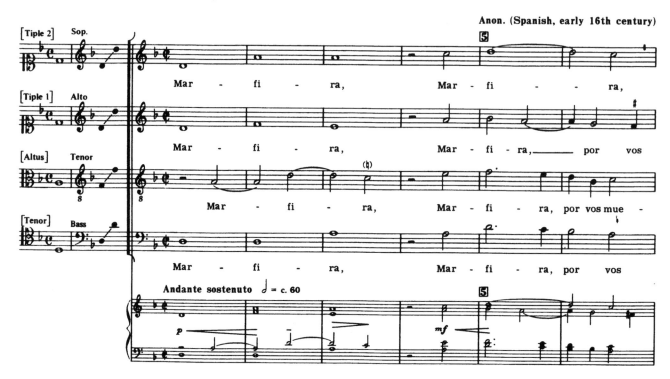

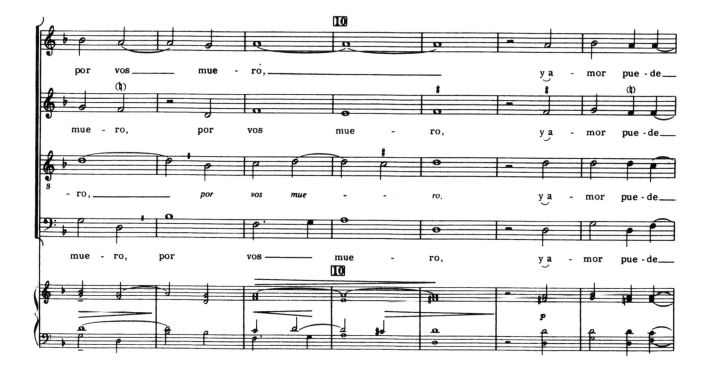

6

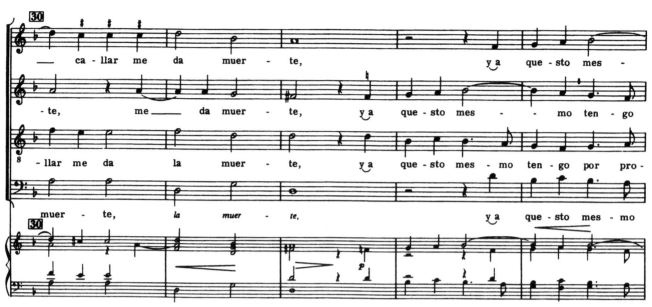

7

8

3. PASA EL AGOA, MA JULIETA

Come across the water, my Lady Julietta. Come to me. I shall go into a garden and pick three roses. My Lady Julietta, cross over the water. Come to me.

Anon. (Spanish, early 16th century)

4. MARGOT LABOUREZ LES VIGNES

Margot, go immediately and till the vineyards. Coming back from Lorraine I met three captains. They told me I was ugly, that I was a very plague to them (a quartain ague).

Jacob Arcadelt (c. 1500–68)

(Verses added from *En Passant par La Lorraine*)
3. Je ne suis pas si vilaine, Puisque le fils du roi m'aime.   3. *I'm not so ugly: the King's son loves's me.*
4. Il m'a donné pour etrenne Un bouquet de marjolaine.   4. *He gave me as a gift a bouquet of marjoram.*
5. S'il fleurit je serai Reine, S'il meurt je perds ma peine.   5. *If it flowers, I shall become Queen; if it dies, my efforts are wasted.*

5. CARISSIMA ISABELLA

Dearest Isabella, your beauty surpasses that of all other women among us, and you have even greater
beauty than the world honours in you. For the divine mind, which ascends to heaven with such swift
flight, values you more, since, descending from the high pole filled with burning ice, it clothes itself
again in mortal flesh, giving proof through you of what it has witnessed in heaven.

Jacob Arcadelt (c. 1500–68)

6. PERRETTE DISAIT JEAN

"Perrette", said John, "your affection is breaking me up: relieve me from this longing that grips me so strongly". Perrette then replied, speaking in a soft voice: "Don't be in such a hurry, John. My husband has gone off to the woods."

Guillaume Costeley (c. 1531–1606)

16

7. BELLISSIMA MIRTILLA
(La Bellezza)

1. Most beautiful Myrtle, you are far brighter than the sun, and with a single sunny ray you set light to a thousand hearts which can live happily every hour for ever in the sparkle of your fire.

2. With your delightful glances you can deal out now life, now death. No one can withstand your valour, and those who want to flee from you always have tardy steps and depart your ardent admirers.

3. Every human eye discerns heavenly beauty on earth in you; and no perfume from the flowers of May can equal your fragrance. Before you, humbled and overcome, Love begs for mercy.

Giovanni Gastoldi (c. 1550 – 1622)

4. Se vinto a te s'inchina
   Chi fu sempre invitto arcier,
   Ben vuol ogni dover
   Che à te Dian tutti honor
   E lodi ognun quella beltà divina
   Per cui languisce, e muor, Fa, la, la.

8. FAIR PHYLLIS

John Farmer (c. 1560 –?)

*If conditions allow, this piece may
be sung a tone higher, in G major.

22

... Soon the music has to
go out of print...

9. MATONA MIA CARA

My darling Madonna, I want to sing a song below your window: I'm a Landznecht and very good company.
You must listen to me, 'cause I'm singing a great song, and I fancy you as much as I do Greek wine
and capon. When I go hunting with my falcon I'll bring you back woodcocks as fat as kidneys. If I
don't know how to dazzle you with fine words it's because I don't read Petrarch and haven't come
across the springs of Helicon. But if I make love to you I won't sleep on the job: I'll keep at it all
night, battering like a ram.

Orlandus Lassus (1532 – 94)

26

10. VEDI L'AURORA

See how Aurora from her golden bed returns the day to mortals; and the sun is already raising its breast above the ocean. She (the dawn) came to part us, hence my grief. If you have more to say, try to be brief and fit your words to accord with the time. (Petrarch, *The Triumph of Death*, II, 178ff.)

Orlandus Lassus (1532–94)

11. NO, NO, NO, NO, NIGELLA

Thomas Morley (1557–1602)

12. SAID I THAT AMARYLLIS?

Thomas Morley (1557 – 1602)

36

13. ADIEU, SWEET AMARYLLIS

John Wilbye (1574 – 1638)

38

14. ACH GRETLEIN

"Ah, Gretlein, come with me over the Rhine." "Get lost, I'm scared you'll drop me in it."
"You have a little bag that can hardly hold three coins." She laughed and said: "Oh no I
haven't".

Stephan Zirler (c. 1518 – 68)

42

15. SEVENTEENTH CENTURY ROUNDS

EDITOR'S NOTES

1. General. This series is a thematic anthology of secular European madrigals and part-songs from the 16th and early 17th centuries. The settings are mainly for mixed four-part choir, but there are also some for three and five voices, and an occasional one for six. Five voices are strongly represented because this was an especially popular number in late 16th century madrigals. By and large, the items present relatively few vocal or harmonic difficulties for the fairly able choir, and where more than four parts are required, they are usually drawn from the upper voices (mainly the sopranos), with the tenor line hardly ever being split.

The term madrigal has been interpreted rather loosely. Besides the contrapuntal part-song, it relates to the frottola, ayre, chanson, lied and the villancico, whether courtly or folk (these all basically being harmonised melodies, often very simply set, and usually repeated for each stanza). More obviously, it encompasses the ballet (a short stanzaic setting in two sections with repeats and fa la las), and the canzonet (a lighter style madrigal normally for a small number of voices). Rounds and catches have also been included because they were obviously an important component of a sing-song or a drinking party, certainly in 17th century England, and their choice of subject matter is very free-ranging. To help make madrigal concerts rather more of a party than a performance, at least two or three of the rounds in each volume have been selected as simple enough to be sung by an audience with or without a visual aid (see section 5, of these notes).

One of the most important features of this anthology is the arrangement by subjects, each volume being devoted to one of the prevalent topics in secular songs, for example, "The Animal Kingdom" (vol. 1), "Love and Marriage" (vol. 2) and "Desirable Women" (vol. 3). This provides not only a new approach to madrigal anthologies but also, more importantly, a focus for the singers and, it is hoped, a comprehensible, appetising programme for the audience. Thus, it should be possible to provide a short concert entirely from one of these volumes, and two halves of a longer concert from any two.

Each volume contains at least twelve part-songs and, on average, half a dozen rounds. About one-third of the texts are in English, but an attempt has been made to provide a representative collection of Italian and French lyrics, and, to a lesser extent, of German and Spanish. The selection combines indispensable popular works with a fair mixture of relatively unfamiliar but attractive and singable pieces. Some thought has also been given to affording a balance between the lively and the reflective, the happy and the sad, for the sake of variety of mood and to help mirror the ups and downs, real or imagined, of Renaissance life and love.

2. Editorial method. As with the Chester Latin Motet series, the Editor has endeavoured to make the volumes suitable for both performance and study. The madrigals are transposed, where necessary, into the most practical keys for ease of vocal range, are barred, fully underlaid in modernised spelling and punctuation, are provided with breathing marks, and have a simplified reduction as a rehearsal aid or as a basis for a continuo. Editorial tempi and dynamics have been supplied, but only in the reduction, leaving conductors free to supply their own according to their interpretation, vocal resources and the acoustics. The vocal range is given at the beginning of each piece, as also are translations for the non-English texts.

To help musicologists, the madrigals are transcribed from the most authoritative sources available. Original clefs, signatures and note values are given at the beginning and wherever they change during the course of a piece. Ligatures are indicated by slurs, editorial accidentals are placed above the stave, and the underlay is shown in italics when it expands a ditto sign, or in square brackets when it is entirely editorial. Where the original contains a *basso continuo* it is included as the bass line of the reduction. Instrumental parts, when they do appear, are transcribed within the relevant vocal lines as well as in the reduction. Finally, each volume contains brief notes on the scope of the edition, the composers, stylistic features of the part-songs, the sources used and editorial emendations.

3. The themes and the lyrics. Though the Renaissance was basically a man's world, women were the focus of attention in a great deal of secular art and music and a vast body of literature, though mainly as objects of desire or paradigms of beauty. In the Petrarchan tradition, which pervades the madrigal, the lady, as in the courtly love convention, is the quintessence of beauty, but aloof, unyielding and often unwittingly cruel to her lovesick adorer. Further, in a mixture of Petrarchanism and Neoplatonism there is a close correlation between physical appearance and character, so that the more beautiful the woman, the more virtuous and therefore the more desirable and less attainable (cf. Angelo's soliloquy on Isabella in *Measure for Measure,* II, ii, 164 ff). What precisely constituted beauty obviously varied from country to country and from artist to artist, as may be seen by comparing the women of say, Boticelli, Leonardo, Titian, Dürer and Rubens. However, some idea of the norm is provided by Agnolo Firenzuolo in the sixteenth century, in a treatise based in part on his observation of the girls of Prato. He expresses a preference (as all artists seemed to) for long, curly, honey-blonde hair; jet black eyes or, failing that, azure blue eyes; a white but not too pallid complexion; a neat ear of pomegranate rosiness; spacious forehead; black, finely arched brows; a softly chiselled, slightly receding nose; a fairly small, evenly shaped mouth; well delineated, even, ivory teeth; a white neck with only a suggestion of the Adam's apple; a fairly broad, well rounded, gently heaving, snow-white bosom; long, slender legs; and a small but adequately fleshed foot.

The madrigalists generally echo Firenzuolo's sentiments, but express them in lavish analogies to nature and the cosmos, whereby the mistress so far transcends the qualities of sun, moon and stars that she is no other than a goddess, or a secularised Virgin Mary. Even those lyrics which seem to satirize the Petrarchan convention turn out to be examples of *sprezzatura,* and Shakespeare's sonnet which opens by declaring: "My mistress' eyes are nothing like the sun" concludes:

> And yet, by heaven, I think my love as rare
> As any she belied with false compare.

Not all the sung expressions of desire for the lovely woman fall within the Petrarchan convention. Some derive from Classical pastoral, where the shepherdess, either wilfully remote or superbly skittish, is wooed by an inept, bird-brained lover in the never-never land of Arcadia. Another Classical source is Ovidian, in which the delights afforded by the lady are more obviously sensual. At the same time, native and vernacular traditions either temper the Petrarchan effusions or adapt their own more naturalistic encomia of the mistress, who, whether a highborn lady or lowbred country lass, whether married or unmarried, is endowed with considerable worldly wisdom and knows how to call the tune.

There are three obviously Petrarchan madrigals in this collection. One of them, *Vedi L'Aurora* (no. 10), derives from the works of the poet himself, and heralds the closing lines of *The Triumph of Death,* in which Laura, having appeared in angelic form to Petrarch in a vision on the night after her death, warns him that if he has anything further to say he must be brief, because she must depart with the dawn. To his pathetic question whether he will live long after her death, she gently tells him that this will indeed be his fate. Laura is the prototype of Petrarchan woman, and the fullness of her significance to the lover is emphasised by the innumerable puns on her name, including "golden", "air", "laurel" and (as here) "dawn". Every detail of her beauty is described at length in the sonnets: her eyes, for example (without which all is night), are the subject even of whole *canzoni*. Above all, and seemingly as a resolution of guilt for doting so much on earthly beauty, Petrarch and his followers seize on the Neoplatonic notion that the loved one is a manifestation of divine beauty. The other two madrigal lyrics which reflect this concept are *Carissima Isabella* (no. 5) and *Bellissima Mirtilla* (no. 7). Their descriptions are so etherial that they convey more the impression of a celestial wonderwoman than a flesh and blood earthbound female.

Less celestial, but still vaguely projected are the women in three madrigals of sighs and tears. In *Marfira* (no. 2), the lover paradoxically expresses his silent suffering very loquaciously, lamenting the pain that the lady kindles in his breast, and the breakdown in communication that his silence causes. The rejected lover in *Adieu Sweet Amaryllis* (no. 13), using execrable Ogden Nash rhymes ("-yllis"-"will is"), goes almost without a struggle and without bitterness – the loved one is still sweet – but he clearly expects that the last goodbye will be meaningful (as Browning's lover hopes: "Who knows but the world may end tonight?"). Nigella's lover (no. 11), by contrast, has had enough. In an appearance of dialogue somewhat akin to the skill shown by John Donne, he rejects any further attempt at entrapment by the wilful girl, his "fa la las" constituting his final dismissal of her (or do they? : cf. Drayton's "Since there's no help").

By marked contrast with these conventional effusions is the remarkable parodic *Matona Mia Cara* (no. 9), where the lover, a drunken German mercenary in Italy, woos in broken Italian his somewhat sluttish madonna (Matona) like a bull in a china shop. He boasts that he knows nothing of Petrarch and has drunk more from the tankard than from Helicon's spring, but, in an apt soldier's metaphor, will deliver the goods like a battering ram. More difficult to place stylistically is the Spanish *Pase El Agoa* (no. 3) which invokes the lovely Julietta. It has a blunt romanticism akin to the quasi-courtly yet folk tradition, and contains two of the stock symbolic elements: a call to cross over the water (cf. "Come o'er the bourne, Bessy, to me", mentioned in *King Lear*) and the gathering of roses in a garden. The mixed style of the lyric is paralleled by the polyglot use of Spanish, French, Italian and Latin.

It is rare to sing through madrigals without tripping over the two extremely flirtatious shepherdesses, Amaryllis and Phyllis (whose names, much to the joy of lyricists, rhyme convincingly in feminine endings). Amaryllis is often deserving of high respect (e.g., in Caccini's song and the Wilbye madrigal mentioned above) and she takes a little more wooing than Phyllis, as in round 15 (iii). She is also usually a little prettier, a fact stupidly blurted out by the lover in no. 12, where "sweet Phyll" seems likely to scratch his eyes out. The propensity of Phyllis to tease and run and then eventually yield after a good chase is demonstrated in *Fair Phyllis* (no. 8).

Lower class wenches make their appearance, especially in the rounds which have a propensity for the bawdy or the risqué. Thus the servant, Susan (unlike the paragon Susanna), is encouraged to be furtive in bestowing her favours on a scoundrelly admirer who delivers the well worn line "thou and I do mean no ill". There is also Joan, who twice appears in the rounds, an honest-to-goodness plain English beauty, whose morals are indeterminate, but whose lips are certainly worth the kissing (unlike those of the "greasy Joan" mentioned in the song in Shakespeare's *Love's Labour's Lost*). Yet another comely country lass, Nan, is the May to whom a January earnestly pleads in his yokel's dialect: "Pratty Naun, bonny Naun, const thoo leuf an aude man?"

Amongst the toughest of the women in this collection are the two German farm girls, Marle (no. 1) and Gretlein (no. 14). Marle, asked to drive her geese into the sweet peas, has heard the request many times before and ends the crisp duologue by virtually telling the man to take a long walk on a very short pier. Gretlein, who is no Julietta, laughingly responds to the suggestive taunt of her would-be lover with an emphatic but equivocal rejection.

Of the French women represented here, the first, Margot (no. 4) is another farm girl who believes herself to be sufficiently attractive to daydream that she is loved by the king's son, though in the estimation of three tried captains from Lorraine (common *dramatis personae* in French folk songs) she is as unappealing as a quartain ague. The second French woman is the only married one in the collection: Perrette, a country girl from the north. She tells her lover not to be importunate: there is plenty of time because her husband has gone off to the woods – an unusual twist to the *Au Joli Bois* tradition mentioned in Volume Two of this series.

4. The music. The first three pieces derive from 16th century anthologies. Like many such items, they are anonymous, but their composers certainly deserve to be known. *Traut Marle* was first published in the famous collection of German songs edited by Georg Forster, and appears in the second volume, published in 1540 under the title, *Der Ander Theil, Kurtzweiliger Gutes Frischer Teutscher Liedlein,* (complete set of copies in the Universitatsbibliothek, Jena). Simple in general concept, it begins in the Dorian mode but mainly shifts between the major and minor of F, the D flat (in the transposed key) lending a touch of bitterness to the girl's exclamation. Dialogue is nicely conveyed through antiphony of paired voices, the technique extending to the drumming "herum, pum, pum". *Marfira* derives from a courtly early 16th century manuscript song book in the Biblioteca de la Casa del Duque de Medinaceli in Madrid (sig. 13230, ff. 131v.-2). In a slow-moving near homophonic style with Aeolian mode to match, the part-song is similar to the simpler works of Martin de Rivaflecha and seems to anticipate Victoria's technique for motets of penitence and meditation, even to the point of using the tenor line for creating and resolving suspensions. Melodic strands move by step in the upper parts, and each section is intensified by climactic repetition of the literary text. It should be noted that if the possibilities for *musica ficta* are ignored, this wonderfully smooth expression of almost controlled pain and grief becomes remarkably chill and sepulchral. The next Spanish piece, *Pase El Agoa*, comes from another manuscript choral book, Cancionero Musical de Palacio, ms. 1335, f. 246v. in the Biblioteca de Palacio, Madrid. It is a lively and frisky love song with a jaunty but haunting melody and strong pulsing triple rhythm as if ensuring that the romantic (if polyglot) lyric will never become sentimental. Since the piece is all too brief, it should be repeated at least once in performance, variety being provided by instruments and solo voices.

The next two pieces are by Arcadelt (biographical details in Volume One) and show his characteristic versatility and economy of means. *Margot Labourez Les Vignes* is a setting of a well known folk tune, of which a more famous version is *En Passant Par La Lorraine*. It first appeared in *Tiers Livres de Chansons*, 1554 (STB part-books in the Bibliothèque Nationale, to be supplemented by the Alto from the 1567 edition in the Bibliothèque Municipale, Bourg). The text was popular and was set by Lassus among others. Arcadelt uses a simple harmony for this rapid chanson, lightening the verses by use of two or three parts, the better characterising the lively and self-possessed girl. The alternation of verse and refrain, though common enough in chansons, is so pleasingly cyclic as to make the ear yearn for endless repetition. Since the original sets only two verses, the remaining three have been supplied from *En Passant Par La Lorraine*. The contrasting madrigal, *Carissima Isabella*, was first published in *Secondo Libro De Madrigali* in 1539 (edited here from the 1591 edition in the British Library). It has a refined and tender melodic movement somewhat similar to that in *Il Bianco E Dolce Cigno* (published in Volume One), though with fewer polyphonic strands. There is quiet and restrained word-painting, with short monosyllabic notes for "con si spedito volo", and a descending melisma in the tenor and a fifth drop in the soprano at "da l'alto polo". The subtle movement from Mixolydian to Ionian mode provides a suitable mood of joy pervaded by rays of celestial brightness.

The next composer, Guillaume Costeley (c. 1531-1606), was born in Normandy. He excelled as a secular composer and keyboard player, becoming court organist to Charles IX of France, a fact proudly proclaimed by the title-page of *Musique De Guillaume Costeley*, 1750 (complete set of copies in Bibliothèque Sainte-Geneviève, Paris), from which *Perrette, Disait Jean* is taken. This is a witty chanson. Its nervous contrapuntal points help convey the furtiveness of the dialogue and the importunacy of the lover, who is assuaged and reassured by the lady in the major cadences.

Roughly one generation later than Costeley is the Northern Italian, Giacomo Gastoldi (c. 1550-1622), who had a varied and successful career as a singer and violist at the Mantuan court and as choirmaster at the local church of St. Barbara, eventually obtaining the coveted post of *maestro di cappella* at Milan cathedral. Although Gastoldi composed a quantity of sacred music, including masses and vesper settings, he is best known for his secular music, in particular, his balletti (form described in the second paragraph of this introduction), which made a great impact in England and were imitated by Morley and Weelkes. His *Balletti A Cinque Voci*, from which *Bellissima Mirtilla* is taken, was published in Venice in 1591, and is now readily available in facsimile, though from the 1593 edition, since the 1591 one does not survive complete. The title-page of the work indicates that the collection could be sung or played on instruments, and was also intended as dance music, hence the relative brevity of each item, the use of repeat sections AA BB, and the frequency of triple time. Entitled *La Bellezza*, the present example is a light extrovert commendation of Mirtilla expressed with tongue in cheek vitality, which is capped by a "fa la la" fanfare both as an acclamation and a call to arms (cf. *Amor Vittorioso*). Though taken as a group Gastoldi's ballets seem lacking in variety, individually they are as delicious as pieces of brightly wrapped *torrone*.

The Elizabethan composer, John Farmer, lived mainly in and around London, though he had a brief spell as organist in Dublin. He completed only one book of madrigals, optimistically entitled, *The First Set of English Madrigals to Foure Voices*, 1599 (complete set of copies in the British Library). Farmer is a lively composer with a knack of recreating vignettes with fine strokes of word-painting. *Fair Phyllis* provides a good example of these qualities. Set in the bright Ionian mode, the opening soprano solo depicts both the lonely Phyllis and the voyeuristic narrator, other company being provided by the sheep in the four-part homophonic "feeding her flocks". After the repeat, which serves to fix the melody and the setting, there follows a bemusing little fugue for the half-hearted search by the shepherds. Then wooer Amyntas appears, the voices being paired as for lovers. His search is energetic: the "up and down" quest over hill is a quaver fugue through a sixth and back in upper voices, while the older shepherds sit back droning in the bass. When Amyntas finds his love the pace steadies in preparation for the joy of kissing, alternating onomatopoeically between triple and duple time. The repeat wickedly alters the meaning of the words (as often in rounds), so that the lovers appear to be "kissing up and down", apparently to the narrator's delight.

The two madrigals by Lassus (biographical details in Volume One), provide an even more striking contrast than the two Arcadelt pieces. *Matona*, published in *Libro de Villanelle, Moresche et Altre Canzoni*, Paris, 1581 (set in Biblioteca dell' Accademia Filarmonica, Verona), is in the style of carnival songs which sometimes poked fun at the Holy Roman Emperor's German mercenaries. This soldier sings a parodic serenade in declamatory style, brashly accompanying himself on the guitar with a "don, diri, don" refrain. The tipsiness and lack of sensitivity of the singer are mirrored in frequent syncopation and sudden changes of chord. The climax is reached in the strident rising phrases of "urtar" and the madrigal ends fittingly in a knell-like coda. For all the stylised coarseness of the song, it still sounds like a serenade, hence performances which make the wooer appear more of a Romeo than a brutish, guttural, freebooter. Lassus' masterly *Vedi L'Aurora* comes from his collection, *Continuation Du Melange*, Paris, 1584 (complete set of copies in the Conservatorio Superior de Musica, Madrid). It combines the warmth and mellifluousness of a love madrigal with the angular expressions of pain which characterise some of Lassus' penitential motets. The tranquil depiction of dawn rising is offset by the agitated quick phrases of anxiety. A passage of lengthened chords, with the lugubrious D flat chord and attendant suspension, points the sorrow of "dole" and is followed by a set of brief, urgent and flurried phrases as the precious moments slip by. There is also a frequent unsettling shift between major and minor.

The influence of Gastoldi on Thomas Morley (biographical details in Volume Two) is clearly to be seen in *No, No, No, No Nigella* (transcribed from the British Library set of *First Book of Ballets to Five Voices*, 1595), which is actually based on the Gastoldi ballet, *Possa Morir Chi T'Ama*. The piece is remarkable for the sudden rush of intricate "fa, la, las" in doubled speed in both sections. These convey the apparently lighthearted defiance of a lover who thinks he is emotionally ready for the break but still suffers from a barely concealed torment, and the progression into slow common time at the end seems heavy-hearted in its affirmation. The other Morley item, *Said I That Amaryllis?* was published in *Canzonets or Little Short Airs to Five and Six Voices*, London, 1597 (complete set of copies in the British Library). Like the first piece it has *bravura*, with a nice sense of self-dramatisation and gentle mockery which reflect both on the speaker and the lady. Speech rhythms are carefully observed and the tempi closely reflect the mood of the words. The Dorian mode is skilfully employed and gives place to G major or minor as the text requires.

John Wilbye (1574-1638) deservedly ranks high among the English madrigalists. He lived a fairly quiet and uneventful life and enjoyed the continued patronage of the Kytsons, residing mainly at Hengrave Hall, Norfolk, their family seat. Wilbye published only two volumes of madrigals, which are characterised by a delicacy of style, translucent counterpoint and a tendency to indulge, like Dowland's works, in the music of tears and lamentation. Unfortunately, the texts often fall far below the quality of Wilbye's settings, though it should also be observed that this is true for many English madrigalists, and the best love poetry often is more appropriate to a more monodic type of setting than the madrigal affords. *Adieu, Sweet Amaryllis*, one of Wilbye's best known pieces, derives from his *First Set of English Madrigals To 3, 4, 5, And 6 Voices*, 1598 (complete set of copies in British Library). It demonstrates even more eloquently than the Farmer madrigal that four parts can more than adequately convey a wide range of effects and a sense of fullness. There is an extremely delicate and subtle development of the two-subject opening with a touchingly plaintive use of the brief rising phrases of farewell. A continual ebb and flow controls the different levels of emotional response, and the conclusion is touchingly quiescent.

The collection of part-songs, ends as it began, with a German folk-setting, *Ach Gretlein*, one of the twenty-two songs by Stephan Zirler (c. 1518-68) included in Georg Forster's collection, appearing in the same volume as *Traut Marle* (*Der Ander Theil*, 1540). Zirler, a composer from Bavaria, was a member of the "Heidelberg School", which included Othmayr, Lemlin and Forster himself, who dedicated his fourth volume of songs to Zirler in 1556. Though only twenty-three of Zirler's songs are extant, they were extremely popular and were imitated by many other composers. *Ach Gretlein* is very similar in construction and rhythmic energy to *Traut Marle,* and begins with antiphonal pairings for dialogue effect in much the same way. The tenor in both has the main melody: in this case it includes the unusual interval of a rising minor seventh, though to begin a new phrase.

The rounds include, inevitably, two from the collections of Thomas Ravenscroft (biographical details in Volume One). *Go to Joan Glover* comes from *Deuteromelia* (1609) and *Joan, Come Kiss Me* from *Pammelia* (1609), both of which works are now readily available in facsimile, with original copies housed in the British Library. As always, the rounds are effective yet simple, melodically convincing, and easy to sing. *Come Amaryllis*, by William Lawes (biographical details in Volume One) was anthologised in Playford's *Catch That Catch Can* 1667, also available in facsimile, with original copy in the British Library. The Lawes rounds are not normally for a large number of voices but are often quite extended and rhythmically interesting. William Webb (c. 1600-1660) is a minor composer, who was also a tenor, lute player and teacher; and, for a short time at least, was a member of the Chapel Royal. Most of his rounds, as this one, appear in Hilton's *Catch That Catch Can,* 1652 (British Library, also facsimile edition). His style in rounds is usually smooth and accomplished, and the texts interesting. Finally, John Hilton the Younger (1599-1657) appears for the first of many times in this series. Most of his life was spent in London, where he became organist at St. Margaret's, Westminster. He published a three-part book of ayres in 1627 (one of which appears in Volume 4) and is best known for composing and editing a large collection of rounds, *Catch as Catch Can*, 1652, mentioned above. Like Ravenscroft he sometimes used dialect texts for his rounds; he has a similar knack of sustaining a fairly plausible melody throughout – though with occasional awkwardness – and provides fairly basic but sonorous harmony.

5. Notes on Programming. Since suggestions for performance have been stated at length in the preceding two volumes, they are merely summarized here.

(i). The madrigals can be supplemented with solo songs on the same theme, e.g., Rossiter's *I Care Not For These Ladies,* Campion's *When Laura Smiles,* Caccini's *Amarilli.*

(ii). Readings can be interspersed with the music, drawn for instance, from the major sonnet cycles (e.g. of Shakespeare, Spenser, Sidney or Constable), or from drama (e.g., *Love's Labour's Lost, Romeo and Juliet,* etc.) or from the prose Romances. The anthologies cited in Volume Two would be of use here. Equivalent anthologies can be obtained for all the other languages used in this collection.

(iii). A cyclorama or screen can be used to project slides of works of art which correspond to the music performed in theme, period, and nationality.

(iv). The audience should be encouraged to join in rounds and songs. In this collection the first two rounds are perfectly suitable for this, and possibly the last one also. The words and music can be projected on the screen used for the slides.

Index of women's names in this volume

Name	Derivation	Item No.
Amaryllis	"refreshing stream"; "sparkling" (Greek)	12, 13, 15(iii)
Gretlein	diminutive of Margareta: "pearl"; "child of light" (Greek)	14
Isabella	variant of Elizabeth: "God's oath"; "dedicated to God" (Hebrew)	5
Joan	variant of Jane: "grace of God"; "gift of God"	15(i) (ii)
Juliet(ta)	diminutive of Julia, fem. form of Julius: "downy bearded" (Latin) thus: "little downyfaced one"	3
Laura	"laurel" (Latin); "cloistered" (Greek)	10
Marfira	Marfila?: "ivory" (Spanish)	2
Margot	form of Margaret: "pearl"; "child of light" (Greek)	4
Marle	Bavarian contraction for Mary: "comely lady" (Hebrew)	1
Matona	German mispronunciation of Madonna: "my lady" (Italian)	9
Mirtilla	Myrtle: "token of victory" (Greek)	7
Nan	Nancy or Ann: "grace" (Hebrew)	15(v)
Nigella	the flower "love-in-the-mist" (Latin); fem. of Nigel (niger): "black" (Latin)	11
Perrette	Pierrette, feminine of Pierre: "rock" (Greek)	6
Phyllis	"a green bough" (Greek)	8, 12, 15(iii)
Susan	"a lily" (Hebrew)	15(iv)

Textual notes and emendations

Marfira, S, 26-7, "es" after "dolor" in orig.; 51-3, "Querria sin hablar" in orig.; A, 38-9, "traygo" em. from "tengo"; 41-2, "vos" em. from "bos"; T, 17-8, "sufro" em. from "amo"; B 6, "vos" em. from "ti"; 20-1, "sufro" em. from "amo"; 23-5, "es" after "si" in orig.

Pase El Agoa, A, 2, D em. from E.

Fair Phyllis, T, 34, 38, 39, C instead of ₵ (all other parts); probably C intended because initial sig. is C.

The Chester Books of Madrigals
Edited by Anthony G. Petti

Chester Music